Been There! ITALY

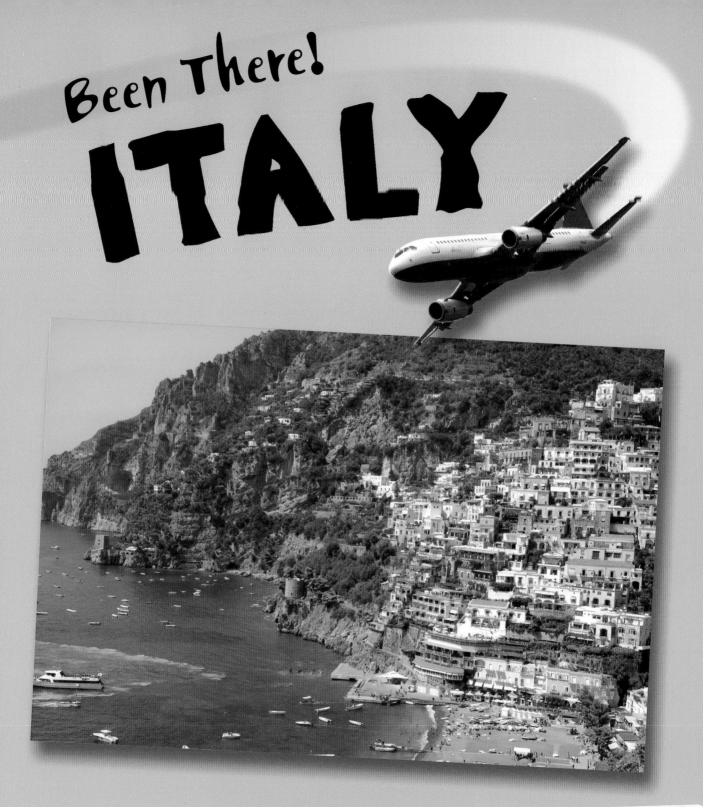

by Annabel Savery

A+

Smart Apple Media

Facts about Italy

Population: 59.1 million

Capital City: Rome

Currency: Euro (€)

Main Language: Italian

Rivers: Po, Arno, Tiber

Area: 116,324 square miles (301,277 sq km)

Published by Smart Apple Media
P.O. Box 3263, Mankato, Minnesota 56002

Printed in the United States of America at Corporate Graphics, in North Mankato, Minnesota.

Library of Congress Cataloging-in-Publication Data
Savery, Annabel.
  Italy / by Annabel Savery.
    p. cm. -- (Been there!)
  Includes index.
  ISBN 978-1-59920-473-4 (library binding)
  1. Italy--Juvenile literature. I. Title.
  DG417.S28 2012
  945--dc22
                        2010043372

Created by Appleseed Editions, Ltd.
Planning and production by Discovery Books Limited
www.discoverybooks.net
Designed by Ian Winton
Edited by Annabel Savery
Map artwork by Stefan Chabluk
Picture research by Tom Humphrey

Picture Credits: Corbis: p11 main (William Manning), p14 (Stefano Amantini), p25 (John Miller), pp26-27 (Guido Cozzi); Discovery Picture Library: p5 middle (Rob Bowden); Getty Images: p5 top (David Madison), p6 top (Venturelli/Contributor), p7 (Michael Freeman), p8 (Panoramic Images), p12 (De Agnostini), p13 (Deboragh Lynn Guber), p18 (Herve Hughes), p23 (Tim Macpherson); Istockphoto: p11 inset (AccesscodeHFM), pp20-21 (Flory), p28 (prluka); P. Humphrey: p16; Shutterstock: title page & p22 (Natalia Baruskova), p2 (Route 66), p6 bottom (Phillip Minnis), p9 top & p30 (Peter Wey), p9 bottom (yykkaa), p10 & p31 (Sailorr), p15 (Schalke fotografie / Melissa Schalke), p17 (Chad Buchanan), p19 top (Gasper Furman), p19 (Rostislav Glinsky), p24 (Malgorzata Kistryn), p27 inset (Aneta Skoczewska), p29 (Colman Lerner Gerado).

Cover photos: Shutterstock: main (Luciano Mortula), left (Evitta), right (Jonathan Larsen).

DAD0046
3-2011

9 8 7 6 5 4 3 2 1

Contents

Off to Italy!

We are going on a vacation to Italy. This is a country in the south of Europe. It is shaped like a high-heeled boot.

Two large islands are part of Italy, too. They are called Sicily and Sardinia. You can see them on the map. The arrows on the map show the different places we will visit.

We are visiting in summer, so it will be hot. But it might still be cool in the evenings or when we visit the mountains.

Here are some things I know about Italy . . .

- Foods that originally came from Italy, such as pizza and pasta, are eaten all over the world today.

- Many famous artists, such as Michaelangelo and Leonardo da Vinci, come from Italy. Their art is displayed all over the world.

- Italy is a peninsula. It sticks out into the Mediterranean Sea and is surrounded by water on three sides.

On our trip I'm going to find out lots more!

Arriving in Milan

We arrive in Milan in the afternoon. Outside the airport, the air is hot and sticky.

Milan is a big city in the north of Italy. Many people live and work here. Every year, big fashion shows are held here in the spring and fall.

For my first meal in Italy, I have **risotto**. It is like a savory rice pudding with herbs and mushrooms. It is lovely and creamy.

After lunch, we go to see the *Duomo*. This is an enormous cathedral. You can go up and walk on the roof. The view is amazing. The guidebook says that on a clear day, you can see a range of mountains called the Alps.

The *Duomo* is the largest Gothic cathedral in the world. It took 500 years to build.

Mountains and Lakes

From Milan we travel by train to Lake Garda.

First, we have windsurfing lessons on the lake. It is lots of fun, but the water is cold when we fall in.

Our instructor says this is the largest lake in Italy. At the south, it is wide and the land is flat. To the north, the lake is narrower and surrounded by craggy mountains.

The next day we go hiking in the Dolomites. This is the name for the eastern part of the Alps.

The highest parts of the mountains are jagged and rocky. Lower down, there are lots of wild flowers and bright green grass. In the winter, these slopes are covered with snow, and people ski here.

Golden eagle

The area we are in is a national park. These are areas where wild animals and their **habitats** are protected.

The Floating City

From the Dolomites, we travel east all the way to the sea at Venice.

Vaporetto

Dad says that Venice is built on 117 islands that are separated by canals. Everyone in Venice travels by water. We take a water bus called a *vaporetto* down the Grand Canal to the *Piazza San Marco*.

The piazza is the main square. It is in front of the church of Saint Mark, or the *Basilica di San Marco*. This is one of the most famous places in Venice and is very crowded with people.

In the narrow streets around the piazza, people sell carnival masks and Venetian glass.

Venice is a very old city. For hundreds of years, it was an important port for people trading between Europe and eastern countries, such as China and India.

Fabulous Florence

Today we take the train from Venice to Florence. On the way we cross the Po River.

The river brings water to the surrounding land, which makes this area good for farming. Crops, such as wheat and rice, are grown here.

To get to the city center from our hotel, we have to cross the *Ponte Vecchio*. This is an old bridge over the Arno River. There are jewelry shops all along the sides of the bridge.

Ponte Vecchio

We walk on to find the *Palazzo Vecchio*. This is Florence's town hall. It looks more like a castle to me.

On the way, we stop at a *gelateria*. This is an ice cream shop. The ice cream is made right there in the shop. There are all sorts of flavors to choose from. I choose the bright green pistachio ice cream. Yum!

In the Countryside

Before leaving Florence, we go to the Uffizi art gallery. We are in a line for a long time, but it's worth it. Many famous artists have lived and worked in Florence. There are 45 rooms full of art here, so it takes a long time to look around.

In the afternoon, we rent a car and drive up into the hills. Mom has found a villa where we can stay. It has stone walls and an orange tiled roof.

We are in the region of Tuscany. The hills are green, and there are rows of thin trees that Dad says are called cypress trees. There are vineyards with grapevines planted in rows, and we also see olive trees with silvery leaves.

After two days here, we set off for Rome.

Exploring the Capital

Rome is Italy's capital city. Lots of people come to visit the city each year. There are old buildings that have been here for a long time, and there are also new, modern buildings.

When we get to the city center, it is busy and noisy. Drivers are beeping their horns at each other, and there are scooters whizzing around. A policeman blows his whistle very loudly to direct traffic.

There are lots of sights to see in Rome. My favorite is the Trevi Fountain. In the center is the sea god Neptune, and on either side are horses that are pulling his chariot in the sea.

In the evening, we go to a restaurant. It is busy, and lots of people are eating and laughing together. We eat pasta shaped like ribbons in tomato sauce. It is delicious.

The Eternal City

Rome is known as the "Eternal City" because it is so old. More than 2,000 years ago, people called the Romans ruled a great empire, and Rome was its center.

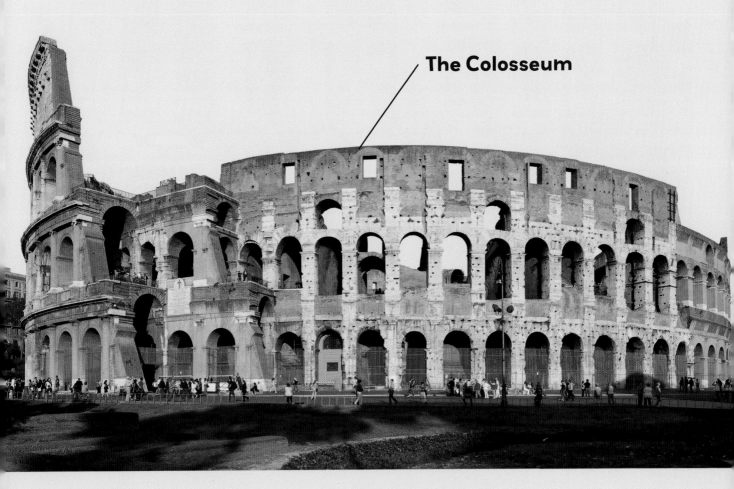

The Colosseum

Many buildings that the Romans built are still standing today. One is the Colosseum. It is an enormous oval arena. Romans would watch entertainment here, such as **gladiator** fights.

On our last day in Rome, we go to Vatican City. This is where the Pope lives. He is head of the Roman Catholic Church. Most people in Italy are Catholics.

There is a wall around Vatican City that separates it from the rest of Rome. This is because it is a different country and even has its own postal service and army (below).

Next Stop . . . Naples

I am looking forward to going to Naples, since my teacher told me that this is where pizza was invented. At the *pizzeria*, they have a **wood-burning oven** for cooking the pizzas.
My pizza has tomatoes, olives, ham, and cheese on it.
Yum!

Near Naples is a huge volcano called Mount Vesuvius. We walk up to see the big crater at the top. On the way, we pass more olive trees and vines.

Mount Vesuvius

A Preserved City

In 79 BC, Mount Vesuvius erupted. The lava and hot ash from the eruption covered the cities of Herculaneum and Pompeii.

Many hundreds of years later, scientists discovered that the city of Pompeii was still there under the rock. Since then, they have uncovered the remains of the ancient city.

The Amalfi Coast

Next, we travel south to the Amalfi Coast. We are staying in a hotel near the small town of Amalfi.

The road winds back and forth. On one side is a high cliff side and on the other, the land drops steeply into the sea. The drive is quite scary.

The hotel owner is named Catarina.
Her family lives nearby and helps her
to run the hotel. I took this photo of
some of them.

Catarina's oldest daughter, Bianca, goes
to school in Amalfi. She has to get up
early because class starts at 8:30 a.m., but
she finishes at 2:00 p.m. In the afternoon,
she helps her mom or goes to the beach.

At the Market

For a few days, we are going to travel around southern Italy. This is a big region, but there are fewer cities than in the north.

In one town, we go to a bustling market. All the stalls are selling different foods. Mom says that they have all been grown or made nearby.

There are lots of types of bread and cakes. Fruit stalls are piled high with oranges and lemons. There are bright red tomatoes and purple eggplant.

At the cheese stall, a man gives us some cheese to taste. Nearby, a woman is selling olive oil.

Over the Sea to Sicily

When we get to the city of Reggio di Calabria, we are right at the toe of the boot of Italy. We get on a ferry to cross the Straits of Messina to Sicily.

We are going to take the train from Messina to the island's capital city of Palermo.

Did you know that Sicily was once part of Greece? You can still see Greek temples near the city of Agrigento.

The railroad runs along the Tyrrhenian coast. The sea is bright blue, and there are lots of small, rocky coves and misty islands.

In Palermo, we go to a little street café. Sicily is famous for pastries and desserts. We try *cannoli*. These are pastries stuffed with **ricotta** cheese and covered with chocolate. Fantastic!

Sparkling Sardinia

Sardinia is the final place we are going to visit. There is one boat a week from Palermo to Cagliari, Sardinia's capital city. The journey takes 13 hours.

In the city, there are lots of old buildings as well as new ones. We climb up inside an old tower called the *Torre San Pacrizo*. From the top, we can see the old town and the port. People look very small and busy from up here.

On the northeast coast of Sardinia is an area called *La Costa Smeralda*, or "the Emerald Coast." This is a popular vacation spot for wealthy people.

Before we leave, we travel inland to see the *nuraghi*. These buildings were built when the **indigenous** people of Sardinia lived here between 1500 and 500 BC.

From Cagliari, we travel back to Milan to catch our flight home. I can't wait to tell my friends about our trip to Italy!

My First Words in Italian

Buon giorno (*say* **Bwohn johr-noh)**   Hello

Arrivederci (*say* **Ah-ree-vay-dehr-chee)**   Goodbye

Come stai? (*say* **Koh-meh stah-ee)**   How are you?

Come ti chiami?
(*say* **Koh-may tee kee-ah-mee)**   What is your name?

Mi chiamo Sandra.
(*say* **Mee kee-ah-moh Sandra)**   My name is Sandra.

Counting 1 to 10

1 **uno**   (*say* **oo-noh**)   6 **sei**   (*say* **sah-ee**)
2 **due**   (*say* **doo-ay**)   7 **sette**   (*say* **seh-tay**)
3 **tre**   (*say* **tray**)   8 **otto**   (*say* **oh-toh**)
4 **quattro** (*say* **kwat-roh**)   9 **nove**   (*say* **noh-vay**)
5 **cinque** (*say* **sink-way**) 10 **dieci**   (*say* **dee-ay-see**)

Words to Remember

gladiator a person in ancient Rome who fought other people or animals to entertain an audience

Gothic a style of architecture

habitat the place where an animal lives

indigenous originating from, or native to, a particular country or region

peninsula a strip of land that is almost completely surrounded by water

ricotta a soft, white cheese made with sheep's milk

risotto a thick rice dish, with meat, fish, seafood, or vegetables added

wood-burning oven an oven that uses wood for fuel

Index

Learning More about Italy

Books

Focus on Italy (World in Focus) Jen Green, World Almanac Library, 2007.
Looking at Italy (Looking at Countries) Jillian Powell, Gareth Stevens, 2007.
Italy (Exploring Countries) Walter Simmons, Bellwether Media, 2011.
Welcome to Italy (Welcome to the World) Mary Berendes, Child's World, 2008.

Web Sites

Geography for Kids, Geography Online, and Geography Games
   http://www.kidsgeo.com/index.php
National Geographic Kids, People & Places
   http://kids.nationalgeographic.com/kids/places/find/italy
SuperKids Geography directory, lots of sites to help with geography learning.
   http://www.super-kids.com/geography.html